Par fo   ?

Golf Jokes,
101 hilarious
random jokes, puns,
and one-liners!

I've seen better swings on a porch!

The only thing
that causes more cheating
than golf is income taxes.

My wife dreamt that moose
were falling from the sky. I
told her, it's just reindeer.

I went to the zoo and saw a
baguette in a cage. The
zookeeper said it was bread in
captivity.

The golfer looked at his caddie and said, "I've played so badly all day, I think I'm going to drown myself in that lake." The caddie, quick as a flash, replied, "I'm not sure you could keep your head down that long."

Did you hear about the guy that evaporated? He'll be mist.

Golf can best be defined as an endless series of tragedies obscured by the occasional miracle.

I used to be a shoe salesman, until they gave me the boot.

Will glass coffins be a success? Remains to be seen.

A little girl was at her first golf lesson when she asked an interesting question..."Is the word spelled P-U-T or P-U-T-T?" She asked her instructor. "P-U-T-T is correct," the instructor replied. "P-U-T means to place a thing where you want it. "P-U-T-T means merely a futile attempt to do the same thing."

What is the difference between a golfer and a fisherman? When a golfer lies, he doesn't have to bring anything home to prove it.

What did the librarian say when the books were a mess? We ought to be ashamed of ourshelves.

I told my buddy I got a new set of clubs for my wife. He said, "Sounds like a good trade!"

Accidentally buried someone alive. It was a grave mistake.

Yeah, I steal brake fluid. But I can stop anytime.

I shot one under at golf today. One under a tree, one under a bush, and one under the water

This girl thought she recognized me from vegetarian club, but I've never met herbivore.

I'm glad I learned sign language. It's really handy.

Golfer to caddie: "Why do you keep looking at your watch? I find it very distracting."

Caddie: "It's not a watch, sir – it's a compass."

You should wear glasses while doing math. It improves division.

My wife told me to stop speaking in numbers. But I didn't 1 2.

In golf, you can hit a 2-acre fairway 10-percent of the time, but hit a 2-inch branch 90-percent of the time.

My friend's bakery burned down. Now his business is toast.

My kid swallowed some coins, the doctor told me to just wait. No change yet.

In primitive society, when native tribes beat the ground with clubs and yelled, it was called witchcraft; today, in civilized society, it is called golf.

I'm designing a reversible jacket. I'm excited to see how it turns out.

I had a joke about amnesia, but I forget how it goes.

"My wife was wearing sexy lingerie... she said I could tie her up and do whatever I wanted. So I tied her to the chair and went to the driving range."

I suffer from kleptomania. But I take something for it.

I met my wife on a dating site. We just clicked.

In golf, some people tend to get confused with all the numbers... they shoot a "six", yell "fore" and write "five".

I was worried about being in a long-distance relationship. But so far so good

My boat was cold, I tried to make a fire but it sank. I guess you can't have your kayak and heat it too.

How many golfers does it take to change a lightbulb? Fore.

Just found out sticks float. They would.

What does C.S. Lewis keep in his wardrobe? Narnia business.

Please don't make my funeral too early. I'm not really a mourning person.

If I hit it right, it's a slice. If I hit it left, it's a hook. If I hit it straight, it's a miracle.

Yesterday a clown held the door open for me. It was such a nice jester.

An atom lost an electron. It really should keep an ion them.

Becoming a vegetarian is a big missed steak.

What's the easiest shot in golf? Your fourth putt

I went to a new mechanic. They came highly wreck-a-mended.

My ceiling isn't the best, but it's up there.

Wife: You spend far too much time concentrating on golf! Do you even remember the day we got engaged? **Husband:** Sure I do. It was the same day I shot even par.

After a particularly poor round, a golfer spotted a lake as he walked despondently up the 18th. He looked at his caddie and said, "I've played so badly all day, I think I'm going to drown myself in that lake." The caddie, quick as a flash, replied, "I'm not sure you could keep your head down that long."

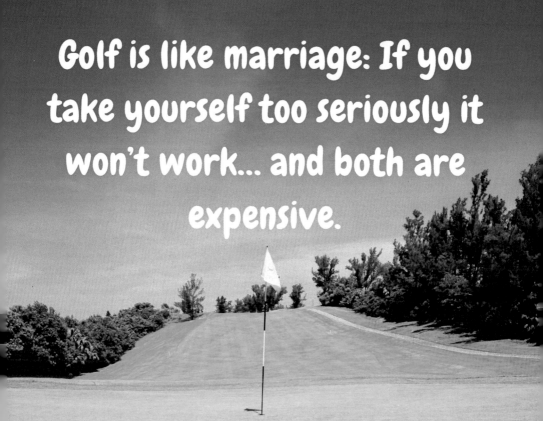

Golf is like marriage: If you take yourself too seriously it won't work... and both are expensive.

Clones are people two.

Did you hear about the silk worm race? It ended in a tie.

I once had a teacher with a lazy eye. She couldn't control her pupils.

There are three ways to improve your golf game: take lessons, practice constantly... or start cheating.

I used to build stairs for a living. Business was up and down.

Two windmills in a field and one asks the other, "What kind of music do you like?" The other says, "I'm a big metal fan."

The secret of good golf is to hit the ball hard, straight, and not too often.

My new girlfriend works at the zoo. I think she's a keeper.

I put a new freezer next to the refrigerator, now they're just chilling.

"My wife said I play so much golf it's driving a wedge between us."

A short psychic broke out of jail. They were a small medium at large..

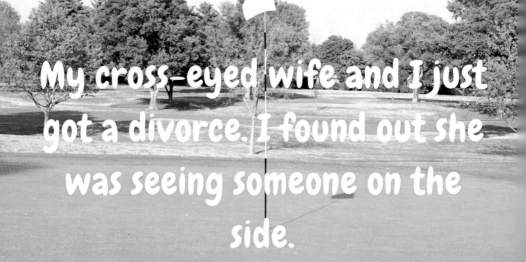

My cross-eyed wife and I just got a divorce. I found out she was seeing someone on the side.

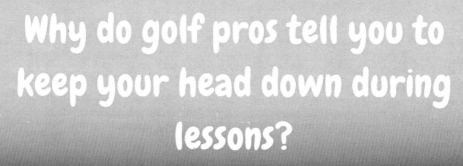

Why do golf pros tell you to keep your head down during lessons?
So you can't see them laughing.

I only hit two good balls today..... when I stood on a rake

A golfer standing at a tee overlooking a river sees a couple of fishermen and says to his partner, "Look at those two idiots fishing in the rain."

I asked my French friend if she likes to play video games. She said, "Wii."

What is heavy forward but not backward? A ton.

To some golfers, the greatest handicap is the ability to add correctly.

Which day do chickens hate the most? Friday.

Golf balls are like eggs. They're white. Sold by the dozen. And a week later you have to buy some more.

If you ever want to talk about why our air conditioning bill is so high, my door is always open.

Two golfers are ready to play on the 11th tee as a funeral cortege passes by. The first player stops, doffs his cap, and bows his head as the cortege passes. "That was a really nice thing to do," the second golfer says. "It's good to see there is still some respect in the world." "Well, it's only right," the first golfer replies. "I was married to her for 35 years."

Why are computers such naturally good golfers? They have a hard drive.

A termite walks into a bar and says, "Where is the bar tender?"

I'm very pleased with my new fridge magnet. So far I've got twelve fridges.

Fairway: An unfamiliar tract of closely mowed grass running from the tee to the green. Your ball is usually found immediately to the left or right of it

I went to see the doctor about my blocked ear. "Which ear is it?" he asked. "2022," I replied.

Golfer: The doctor says I can't play golf. Caddie: Oh, he's played with you, too, eh?

What happened to the lost beef shipment? Nobody's herd.

The best wood in most golfer's bags is the pencil.

A salesman tried to sell me a burial plot. But that's the last thing I need.

There's a disease that makes you uncontrollably tell airport jokes. No cure... it's terminal.

If your opponent can't remember if he shot a six or a seven on a hole, chances are he had an eight on it.

"Is this pool safe for diving? It deep ends."

What do you call a hippie's wife? Mississippi.

An interesting thing about golf is that no matter how badly you play, it is always possible to get worse.

What do you call a boy named Lee that no one talks to?
Lonely

What do you call a magic dog?
A Labracadabrador.

Golfer: That can't be my ball, it looks too old. Caddie: It's been a long time since we started.

My wife asked why I didn't buy her flowers. To be fair, I didn't know she sold flowers.

Most people are shocked when they find out how bad an electrician I am.

The man who takes up golf to get his mind off his work soon takes up work to get his mind off golf.

What do you call a three-footed aardvark? A yardvark

I'm not over the hill. I'm just on the back nine.

Two soldiers are in a tank. One says to the other, "Blubblublubblubblub."

What do you call a dinosaur with an extensive vocabulary? A thesaurus.

You should always try before you buy, especially when buying a putter. Never buy a putter until you've seen how well you can throw it.

What's the king of all school supplies? The ruler.

I hate golf courses with too many trees, I go to great links to avoid them.

A magician was walking down the street – then he turned into a store.

What's the difference between a guitar and a fish? You can't tuna fish.

Why do golfers carry two gloves?
In case they get a hole in one

What's blue and not very heavy? Light blue.

My cat was just sick on the carpet. I don't think he's feline well.

Question: "What did you get on your last hole?"
Answer: "Depressed"

I accidentally rubbed ketchup in my eyes. I now have Heinzsight.

What's Forrest Gump's computer password? 1forrest1